MW00463560

you're the best thing under my tree

by max & lucy®

Time Warner Books

WARNER BOOKS

An AOL Time Warner Company

© Max & Lucy, LLC. All rights reserved.

Many of the pages in this book are based on other Max & Lucy products, including The 12 Nips of Christmas® and Holiday Hide-A-Notes®.

Nips®, Hide-A-Notes®, Max & Lucy®, A Very Stylish Girl®, woof! dog, lil' angel, lil' devil, flat baby and all related titles, logos, characters and artwork are trademarks and service marks of Max & Lucy, LLC.

www.maxandlucy.com

All rights reserved. This publication may not be reproduced in whole or in part by any means whatsoever without written permission from the copyright owners. Permission is never granted for commercial purposes.

Time Warner Books are published by
AOL Time Warner Book Group
1271 Avenue of the Americas
New York, N.Y. 10020

 An AOL Time Warner Company

10 9 8 7 6 5 4 3 2 1
ISBN:1-931722-13-7
Printed in the United Kingdom

it's that time of year again

We're suckers for the holidays. Sure, we get stressed out each year, but we find ourselves with the holiday music on and our spirits a little more hopeful anyway. And sometimes, if we get a minute or two at night, usually by ourselves, we reflect on just how lucky we are.

If you're reading this, you're either about to share this little book with someone you care about, or you received it from someone who cares about you.

The fact that either one of those possibilities has happened is something to celebrate. Which is exactly what this little book is about. So grab a comfy chair, pour a nice hot toddy or cup of tea, and delight in the holiday season.

max & lucy®

a few holiday thoughts
of your own

you're the best thing
under my tree...

...because...

without you, i'd be a drift

you make my wishes come true

to me, you're purr-fect

i checked my list,
you're on it twice

i'm thankful
you're part of my world

merry christmas, baby

pssssst, thinking of you
for the holidays

you crack me up...

...no wonder i'm nuts about you

We're a pair

twisted and sweet,
that's why i like you!

i'd like to mistle you
from head to toe!

i'd fetch any present for you

i'll never forget you

you make me twinkle

have a very stylish christmas

you're one-of-a-kind

the holidays are in the bag
when i'm with you

you top my tree

you sleigh me

you add spice to my holidays...

...and make any home sweet!

let's hang together

you make me feel like a star

merry chris-mouse!

you're a priceless gift

i'm not always an angel,
but you are

your roof? or mine?

let's cut out and get merry!

i'm a hog for egg nog!

with you, all is bright

you make me warm

merry christmas...

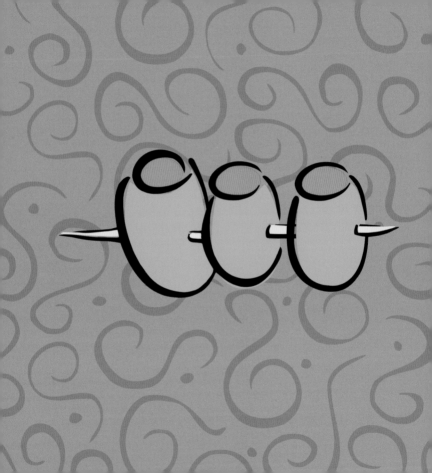

...and a happy new year!

you're the best thing
under my tree

acknowledgments

The entire staff at Max & Lucy helped make this book possible, and we thank them all. We offer special acknowledgment to Bradley Smith and Aaron Thompson for their witty designs and perpetual can-do attitudes. To our families and friends who continue to believe in us, we share our gratitude. And, of course, to our friends at AOL Time Warner Books, who made this entire project possible, we send our deepest appreciation.

max & lucy

about max & lucy

Max & Lucy is a tiny little company in Phoenix, Arizona, that makes
greeting cards, notes and other fun ways for people to correspond.
Founded by Russ Haan and named after two cats who live in a ware-
house, the company is now owned by Russ and two good friends,
Mike Oleskow and Bradley Smith. As the author in the crowd, Russ
penned most of this book, but humbly admits that without his
partners, the words would not have been the same. To learn more
about Max & Lucy, feel free to visit the company's web site at
www.maxandlucy.com.

max & lucy®